This page intentionally left blank.

This page intentionally left blank.

Modern Trade Theory -- Belt and Road Initiative Study Case

by

Yunxin Chang

edited by

Lingkai Kong

Modern Trade Theory -- Belt and Road Initiative Study Case

Author: Yunxin Chang. Editor: Lingkai Kong

Istanbul Commerce University, Istanbul, Türkiye

Izmir University of Economics, Izmir, Türkiye

changyunxin@outlook.com

* * * * * * * * * * * * * *

* * * * * * * * * * * * * *

ISBN: 978-1-7393257-0-1 (paperback)

Front cover image by Open Democracy & Stettbach Press in Canva

Type set in Kaiti & Canstantia

Published by

Open Democracy & Stettbach Press

Supported by

Acik Demokrasi ve Bilim Vakfi Ltd

(Open D7emocracy and Science Foundation)

219 Kensington High Street, Kensington, London W8 6BD

https://www.opendemocracyfund.org

MODERN TRADE THEORY -- BELT AND ROAD INITIATIVE STUDY CASE

This page intentionally left blank.

为了人类命运共同体。

This page intentionally left blank.

Content

THE AUTHORS

Yunxin Chang 常芸鑫. She received her B.S. and M.S. degrees in Accounting from Zhengzhou University, China, and Uppsala University, Sweden, respectively. She is currently pursuing her PhD in International Trade at Istanbul Commerce University.

As an associate member of ACCA Association (the Association of Chartered Certified Accountants), she is an experienced accounting and financial management professional who has worked for PwC, CITIC Construction, Baker Tilly and other accounting and auditing firms. Currently she is working in Huawei Turkey as a financial controller. She serves as a shareholder and investor in several companies. She is also a research associate at the Istanbul Institute of Political Strategy. She speaks Chinese, English and Turkish.

Lingkai Kong. A PhD candidate in Political Science, Izmir University of Economics, Turkey. He received his bachelor degree in Economics from Beijing Foreign Studies University, China, and master degree in Economics from the University of Zurich, Switzerland.

He is the author of the book *The Philosophical Reviews of International Politics*. He translated and edited the books "Luo Zhi Jing" - *Classic of Accusation,* and "Zhi Xue" - *Classic of Self-restraint,* into English version for the first time. He also retranslated and edited the English version of the book *The Art of War* to make it more accurate and readable, and substantially revised the Lionel Giles's version that was in circulation. He is the manager of the *Journal of Politics and Strategy* and co-founder of the Acik Demokrasi ve Bilim Vakfi (Open Democracy and Science Foundation). He is a reviewer and editorial board member for several journals.

This page intentionally left blank.

ACKNOWLEDGEMENT

Thanks to Prof. Dr. Üyesi Cihat Köksal for the excellent course. The main content of this book is adapted from the course papers of his "International Trade Theory" course. Thanks to Istanbul Commerce University for providing a good learning platform and academic atmosphere.

Thanks for the support from Acik Demokrasi ve Bilim Vakfi (Open Democracy and Science Foundation). Thanks for Open Democracy & Stettbach Press to edit and publish this book.

This publication is available in paperback format with ISBN 978-1-7393257-0-1, and also available in e-book format on several platforms. Readers are welcome to point out any errors.

If you have any questions, or the possibility of cooperation, please contact: changyunxin@outlook.com

This page intentionally left blank.

PREFACE

Within the realm of international trade, contemporary ideas are evolving and expanding in step with the changing times in order to maintain their capacity to provide an explanation for modern-day global business. The "Belt and Road Initiative" (BRI) project, which was recently presented by China in 2013, has drawn a lot of attention and controversy since it is a big initiative of international commerce that covers more than 140 nations. By employing emerging evidence and conducting a literature study on relevant topics, the purpose of this research is to investigate the economic implications and motivations behind BRI. We came to the conclusion that China had specific motivation for proposing the BRI in 2013, including the accumulation of capital, the export of infrastructure, market access, the solution to the problem of unbalanced growth, the guarantee of an energy supply, and the creation of a stable border environment. In addition, contemporary theories, particularly the economics of scale, technological gap, overlapped demand, and product life cycle, are ideally suited to explain the reasons for China's actions. In the meantime, the worldwide economy in

2013 had a weak expansion and wanted a stimulant for active global commerce, which made it easier to propose the BRI. In addition, a review of the relevant research reveals that the BRI would have a beneficial effect on the economies of the countries participating in the initiative as well as the global economy overall, although having varying degrees of significance for individual nations.

Current projections in the literature concerning the economic consequences of BRI are based on a variety of models. This is due to the fact that BRI is not completely down-to-ground. When we take a look at the real world, we discover that there are voices in the international community that are both supportive and sceptical, which indicates that the BRI is going to face a number of obstacles. The problem of mounting debt and the ongoing COVID–19 epidemic have been cited as two important issues. Yet, chances and difficulties often go hand in hand with one another. We believe that a prosperous vision will continue be highly respected despite the fact that BRI has a large number of potential chances behind it. It is anticipated that in the not-too-distant future, there will be a rise in international collaboration regarding sophisticated technologies, green economies, educations, and other topics.

1. Introduction

Over the course of several decades, theories about international commerce and economics have progressed in an effort to provide an explanation for the steadily rising levels of human production and the expansion of trading channels around the globe. Theories of international trade have been evolving since the time of the Mercantilists in the 16th century, who believed that international trade was a zero-sum game in which one could either win or lose. These theories include factor endowment theory, absolute advantages in the 17th century, comparative advantages in the 19th century, and Heckscher-Ohlin Theory in the 20th century, among others. In the most recent decades, contemporary theories of international commerce have been significantly improved by the addition of a vast deal of material drawn from a variety of sources. Intra-industry trade, for instance, is intended to describe a novel trading phenomena in which nations purchase and export items belonging to the same industry in order to maintain the reliability of their supply (Scott, 1975). In a similar manner, in order to keep up with the rapid advancement of technology, the concept of the technological gap was developed as a means of comparing the relative strengths of various nations in terms of their ability to innovate (Posner, 1961). A wealth of illuminating ideas provide us with a deeper comprehension of the dynamics at play in today's world economy regarding international commerce. In particular, a recent large project known as the "Belt and Road Initiative," which is shortened as BRI, is a great example of how international ideas may be applied to explain. On his travels in Kazakhstan and Indonesia in 2013, Chinese President Xi Jinping first floated the idea of the Belt and Road Initiative (BRI). Both the land silk road and the marine silk road are often referred to as "one belt" and "one road," respectively. The Belt and Road Initiative (BRI) is a gigantic multi-national initiative that will include more than 65 nations, almost 4.4 billion people, and roughly 30 percent of the world's Economy (Zhai, 2018).

> *"Nations have no permanent friends or allies, they only have permanent interests"* (Lord Palmerston, 1848)

The Belt and Road Initiative (BRI), being such a monumental undertaking, has undoubtedly aroused a great deal of attention and controversy among members of the global community. This research contains to the core idea of diverse national interests throughout its analysis of the BRI in order to get a new perspective. It has been determined whether contemporary trade theories are pertinent and appropriate for the purpose of explaining a substantial international commerce initiative known as the Belt and Road

Initiative. This research is to investigate the BRI project and, where appropriate, employ contemporary ideas to conduct an analysis of the BRI.

The following outline constitutes the framework for this research. To begin, the history is investigated in order to discover where it originated from. Second, in order to evaluate various hypotheses, we will follow the lead of numerous contemporary theories and follow their findings. A brief overview of the terminology used in the various current trade theories is presented in the third section. The background of the Belt and Road Initiative (BRI) in China and other areas of the world is outlined in the fourth step to reveal the underlying reasons. In the meanwhile, there are also some theoretical explanations of various reasons stated. Fifth, an illustration of the general structure is provided so that one may get fundamental knowledge of BRI. Sixth, we investigate the feedback and the economic impact of BRI by looking at the material that is already out there. In the seventh part of this discussion, we show the interpretations which include other concerns of economic effect, challenge, and prognosis, are presented. A conclusion is presented at the end of this piece of work to bring together all of the primary arguments that have been presented.

2. History of BRI

In light of the well-known proverb that asserts "Understanding the past may assist to create the future," it is essential to investigate what the old silk routes were and how they influenced the development of humankind's civilization. In the years B.C. 202-138, the emperor of China's Han dynasty sent a man named "Zhang Qian" on an expedition to the west with the hope of discovering other countries (Juping,

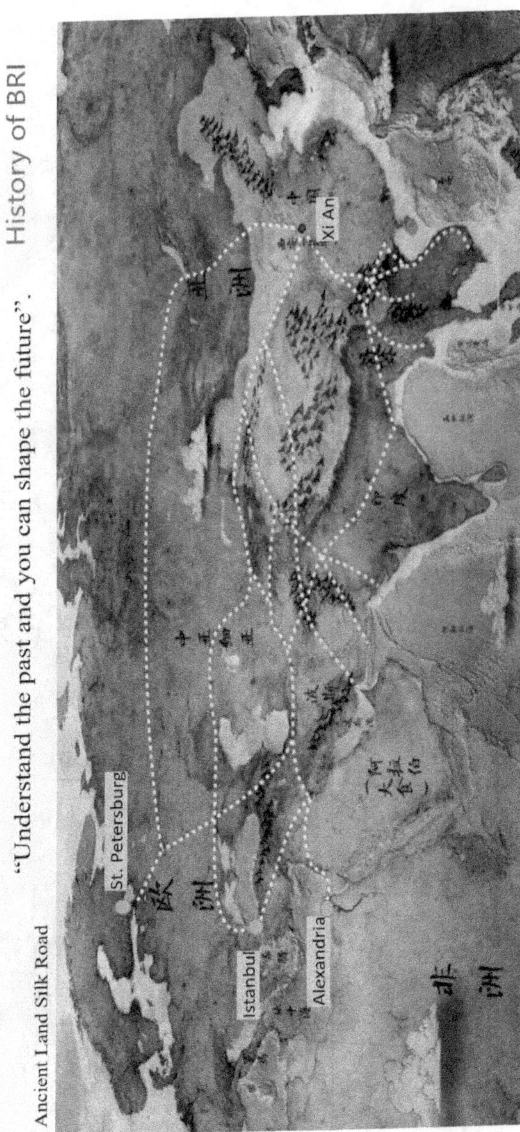

(The map above shows the trade routes of the ancient Silk Road)

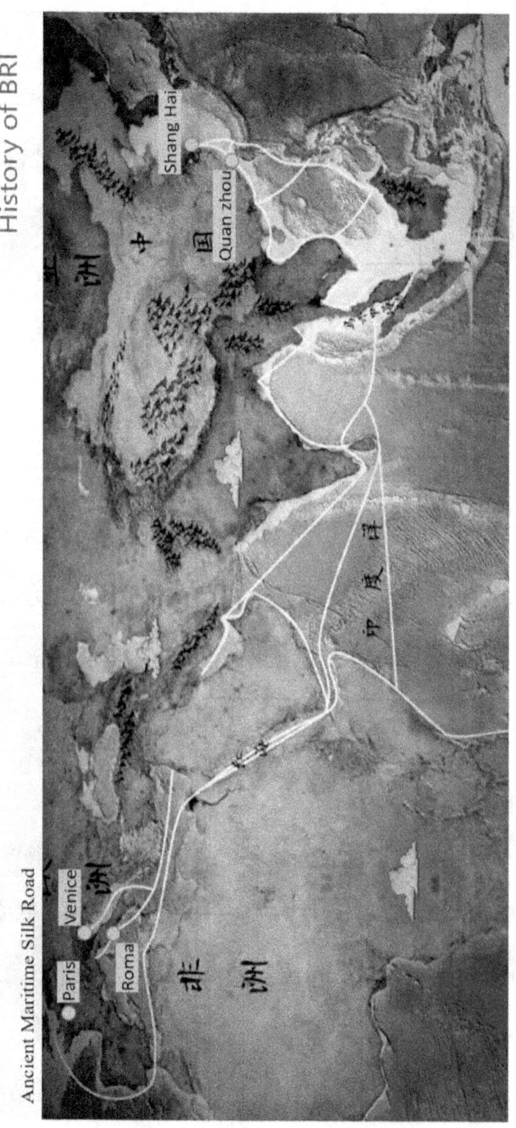

(The map above shows the trade routes of the ancient maritime Silk Road)

2009). It is the first time for the Chinese people to arrive in the Mediterranean region as a consequence of their voyage, and they discovered a whole new world by trekking through land. Together with the enthusiasm of people living in both China and the Mediterranean region, the two-way trade of economic commodities has formed on this route, which makes it easier for people from both regions to communicate with one another. For instance, China sent traditional products such as silk, porcelain, and iron to nations in the Mediterranean, while at the same time, Mediterranean countries supplied China with flax, grapes, and spices through their own trade routes (Juping, 2009). The trading of tangible products led to the gradual expansion into the trading of intangible things such as expertise, cultural traditions, religious beliefs, and scientific knowledge. It has been demonstrated that many of China's religious customs, geographical concepts, and medical sciences were first developed in western countries. On the other hand, western nations learned papermaking, gunpowder production, compass making, and iron smelting from China (Juping, 2009). This ancient land silk road had spanned from the east to the west of the Asian continent, beginning in Xi'an, China, and ending in Istanbul, Turkey, St. Petersburg, Russia, and Alexandria, Egypt. It served as a bridge between these cultural centers and had spanned from the east to the west of the Asian continent. As a result, it is reasonable to assert that the land silk route is of utmost significance for the purpose of connecting and communicating with the countries of the east and west. Yet, this significant route did not receive its name until 1877, when a German geographer by the name of Lichhofen published a book detailing his travels and referred to this route as the "Silk Road" (Dong, 2019).

Later on, when shipbuilding and navigational skills reached a more developed stage, the maritime silk road expanded to encompass all of the major oceans, including the Pacific Ocean, Indian Ocean, Red Sea, Mediterranean Sea, and Atlantic Ocean, and it flourished as a result of trade ships traveling between the different bodies of water (Guan, 2016). Marco Polo, a Venetian trader, arrived in China in 1721 via the nautical route, and he spent more than 20 years traveling around the country. Once he had traveled all the way back to Venice. His adventures were chronicled in the book "The Travels of Marco Polo," which popularized the culture of the Far East (Polo, 1986). It is stated that one of the motives for the great expedition that occurred between the years 13 and 15 was the hunt for money in the kingdoms of the east. As a result, the Maritime Silk Road had a significant impact on the development of history and civilization, particularly in the areas of cultural exchange and the establishment of connections between eastern and western nations.

In the 1930s, a Swedish author by the name of Sven Hedin defined the Silk Road as the path that connected people and continents in the most extensive and meaningful way possible (Chin, 2013). When one considers the past, it becomes clear that both the land and marine silk routes had a significant influence on the economic unification of Asia and the development of civilization all across the world. Nevertheless, because of the colonization of the world and other innumerable battles, the once peaceful silk routes have gradually been fractured and have been washed away by the river of history; in fact, a lot of people do not remember them at all.

3. Modern Theory Review

It is vital to have an understanding of the components and implications of contemporary trade theories that are pertinent in order to have a better application of theory to the BRI. In the next part, pertinent ideas are going to be discussed, such as overlapping demand, imperfect competition, economies of scale, intra-industry trade, technological gap, and product life cycle.

Why do nations desire to take part in the global trading market? This is the fundamental issue that has to be answered in the field of international commerce. What kind of light do international issues cast on the matter of national interests? The perfectly adequate justification is founded on the concept of "imperfect competition" (Robinson, 1969). In terms of its idea, imperfect competition profiles the features of a monopolistic competitive market, which is constructed on the basis of two assumptions. Specifically, these assumptions are as follows: The first supposition is that all of the competing businesses in the market are able to differentiate their offerings from those of their competitors. The second supposition is that every firm just accepts the price that its competitors set as a given since, because to information inequity, they are unable to access the components of their competitors' prices. According to these hypotheses, the number of businesses is increasing in tandem with the expansion of the market. Several businesses are forced to engage in cutthroat competition with one another in order to secure a consumer and increase their share of the market. These businesses do this by offering a wider selection of goods at more affordable costs. Customers stand to gain the most from this circumstance, but businesses also stand to profit from it. In all honesty, the profitability of businesses is rather low, but the profits are quite sustainable if there is consistent expansion into new markets. Putting the theory into reality, the theoretical scenario is pretty similar to the actual worldwide trading that takes place since the information that is available on the real market is likewise flawed. In spite of the fact that two assumptions are not valid, the ways in which a larger market benefits both firms and customers are true in the actuality of the situation. As a result, on the supply side of the equation, consumers feel optimistic about global commerce. Also, on the supply side, businesses are keen to engage in the massive global market in the hopes of sustaining their earnings there. Because of this impetus, international commerce is not only possible but also growing.

3.1 Economies of Scales

When entering new markets throughout the world, businesses need to develop competitive advantages that will allow them to survive the rigors of natural selection, which may be rather harsh. Because of this, it is necessary for businesses to devise novel designs or provide competitive prices in order to attract clients. The economies of scale hypothesis is advantageous for a corporation that wishes to cultivate its cost advantage over its competitors. The economic principle known as "economies of scale" states that there is a correlation between increased production volume and a reduction in the average cost of a single unit of output brought about by increased productivity (Stigler, 1958). For instance, in the streamlining of production, the vast number of repetitive tasks that workers are required to do build their learning curves, which in turn lifts their levels of efficiency.

Because of the decreased cost, businesses are able to produce items that are more cost-effective than those of their competitors.

3.2 Intra Industry Trade

The academic community has discovered an interesting phenomena by doing research on the structure of nations' import and export of commodities. The phenomenon reveals that one country can import and export identical items that are classified under the same industry (Scott, 1975). This type of trading is known as "intra industry trade." For instance, the United States' rate of importing and exporting electronic gear is almost equivalent to one another. The underlying explanation may have to do with the reduced cost of transporting goods when importing from nations that are geographically close by, the variety of the tastes of clients, or seasonal selling. Making use of international commerce is done with the intention of achieving the overarching goal of ensuring a steady supply in a particular sector of the economy.

3.3 Product Life Cycle

In today's society, when everything is moving at such a breakneck pace, innovations are the primary engine that power forward societal progress. If we compare the lifespan of a product to that of a human by focusing on the period during which it is most innovative, we can see that the whole life of a product can be broken down into four stages: innovate, grow, mature, and decline (Vernon, 1992). In most cases, during the initial phase of the process, businesses are required to exercise extreme caution while developing new goods, much like raising children. After then, in the second and third phases, products have the ability to develop on their own and mature as a result of competition. The growing and mature stages are the most lucrative for businesses since this is the period when they may make the most money by selling their wares in an audience that is as large as feasible. At the last stage, when new competitors enter the market with more advanced features, it is inevitable that existing goods will begin to deteriorate and move closer to the end of their useful lives. In the context of international commerce, the growth stage and the mature stage are usually characterized by a significant increase in the volume of goods exported from innovative countries to other nations. This increase is motivated by a desire to maximize profits.

3.4 Technological Gap

The theory of the technological gap follows the same line of reasoning as the product life cycle. According to this theory, a newly developed technology has the potential to grant the nation that innovated it a privilege of competitive advantage on the international market simply due to the early timing of production and exporting (Posner, 1961). This hypothesis explains why nations who are leaders in technological innovation might have a superior performance than other countries that have the same factor endowments as the countries that lead the way in technological innovation. But, this advantage will not last forever. It won't be there for long since ultimately it will be replaced by other nations that have control of the same technology and product on their own.

3.5 Overlapping Demand

Linder has put up a notion, from the point of view of the demand that is involved in international commerce, that nations that share the same demand have greater bilateral trading (Linder, 1961). This is demonstrated to be correct at a later time. It is more likely for nations to trade with other countries whose demand is similar to their own, which results in trades going from affluent countries to wealthy countries and from poor countries to poor ones. For instance, the desire for eating caviar may be shared by a number of rich countries, whereas the want for basic electricity may be shared by a number of impoverished ones. The disparity in their economic circumstances is, without a doubt, the cause of this.

These contemporary ideas are all established within the framework of current international commerce, making them pertinent to a variety of businesses that are involved in global trading. For instance, in regard to the concept of overlapping demand, the European Union is an organization that encompasses numerous developed nations that have wants that are comparable to one another. Another illustration of this would be the

BRICS group, which consists of five emerging countries that all have economically comparable circumstances. In conclusion, the aforementioned theories have established a theoretical basis, which will allow for a more in-depth investigation of the BRI reasons presented in the subsequent texts.

4. Background of BRI

The BRI project is first slated for consideration in the year 2013. At the time in question, there were a great number of emerging nations in existence around the globe. Yet, why is China the only developing nation to make this proposal and not others? How does China's current status compare to that of the rest of the world? In light of the aforementioned inquiries, the next part will investigate the history of BRI.

4.1 China's Situation

To begin, looking at China's progress from the standpoint of its economy, one can see that the country has come a long way since 1978, when the program of "reform and opening" was first implemented. When it comes to the phenomenal growth of the Chinese economy, it is difficult to find a way around this brilliant approach. Even in modern times, China's process of reform and openness has not been completed; rather, it has continued to change and adapt to the country's shifting environment. It is not an exaggeration to claim that, after decades of growth, the ideas of "reform" and "open" are ingrained into the blood of the Chinese country, establishing the perspective of psychology. So, what exactly is the core principle behind the reform and openness policy? The core concept is to do away with the totally planned economy and replace it with a socialist market economy (Rawski, 1995). It started to recognize the validity of private businesses and rural markets, which had a significant impact on the increase in productivity. Many economic zones with substantial governmental incentives have been established in order to improve the ability to attract international investment. In terms of agriculture, the "household contract responsibility" was implemented. This ensures that farmers are able to take use of all of the opportunities that are presented by the lands (Rawski, 1995). For instance, the household is expected to make decisions on whether or not to cultivate the land, raise animals on the land, or just rent it to businesses in order to generate profits and, of course, shoulder all of the responsibility. This provides farmers with a tremendous deal of autonomy, which in turn boosts their output.

The economic repercussions have been quite serious ever since the "reform and openness" procedures were implemented. Throughout the period of 1978-2005, Heston and his colleagues at other institutions found that the Chinese GDP per capita had climbed from 2.7% to 15.7% of the US GDP per capita. The total factor productivity (TFP) has been responsible for explaining 40% of the rise in GDP, whereas it only accounted for 13% of the growth between 1957 and 1978. (Heston et al., 2008). This trend proved unstoppable, and as a result, China moved up to the second spot on the GDP rankings in the world in 2013, only behind the United States. This demonstrates China's economic might, which is necessary for the BRI initiative to be proposed.

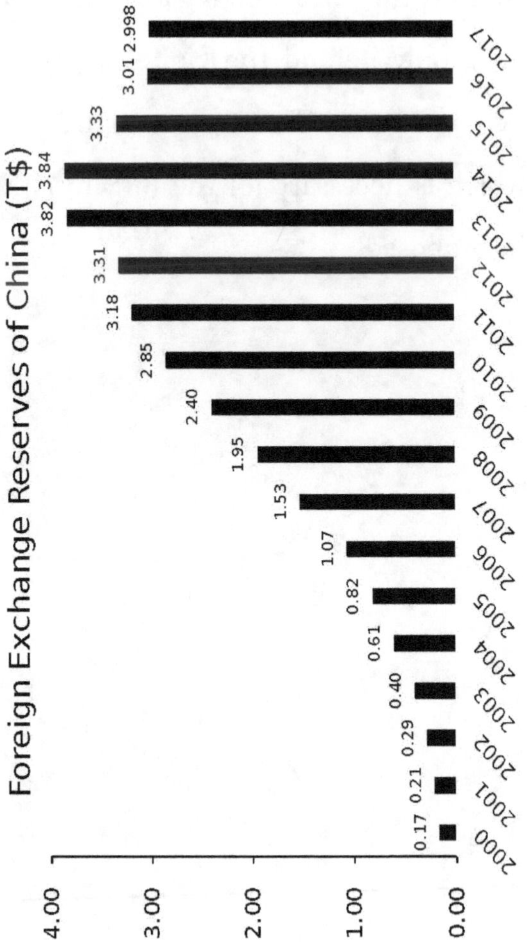

Figure 1: Foreign Exchange Reserve of China 2000-2017.

Second, because the BRI is primarily focused on the export of goods or services connected to infrastructure, it is imperative that an investigation of China's infrastructure capability be conducted in 2013. Back in 2013, the technology used in the development of infrastructures within domestic China, such as metros, high railway trains, bridges, and constructions, was considered to be relatively mature. To give just one illustration, the number of passengers on the high-speed train network increased from 128 million in 2008 to 672 million in 2013 (World Bank, 2014). In addition to the expansion of transportation, China is making significant investments in other types of infrastructure, such as industrial parks, with the goals of enhancing the cluster effects of related industries and developing an environment that is conducive to the development of innovative ideas. According to Bao (2014), there were a total of 1568 industrial parks in China, including those located at the national and municipal levels. To summarize, there have been a lot of significant accomplishments done in the field of infrastructure.

Third, because there has been an increase in the number of novel technologies that have been developed and implemented in the Chinese market, it has resulted in an increase in the overall level of automation. Some examples of this include mobile payment, robot receptionists, and self-checkout supermarkets. The market in China is saturated with available workers, which has led to a cutthroat level of competitiveness among those looking for work. As a result, China has to locate a larger market in order to absorb its surplus of labor and the associated industrial capability.

Fourth, uneven economic circumstances have emerged between China's east and west regions as a direct consequence of the country's fast economic development. The west area, which includes the provinces of Qinghai and Xinjiang, has fallen economically behind Shanghai and Beijing city as a result of the region's plateau climate and rugged terrain. While they make up almost 80% of the country's surface area and 60% of the population as of 2013, the areas in the center and west only contribute for roughly 30% of GDP (Guo, 2014). China, which is a socialist nation, has an overarching goal of achieving widespread wealth. Thus, the Chinese government's primary responsibilities consist of finding solutions to the problem of economic imbalance and enhancing the state of the western regions' economies. This encourages China to turn toward its western neighbors and seek out opportunities to create commercial relationships with those countries. The Belt and Road Initiative (BRI) was established in order to make this vision a reality, given that it is to everyone's advantage for China's western provinces and nations along the BRI to form an economic circle.

Fifth, from the point of view of the nation's energy supply, China is rapidly becoming an industrialized nation, which means that the nation's energy supply serves as the driving force behind the economy. So, from a business perspective, it is important for them to secure the consistent importation of energy from nations that are rich in resources. One example of this would be the importation of gas from Russia and oil from Kazakhstan. These imports necessitate the construction of a significant number of new roads and railways, in addition to an improvement of the associated infrastructure in order to reduce the costs of transportation.

Sixth, with regard to the matter of safety, advancements call for a social environment that is unchanging. Under the Belt and Road Initiative (BRI), China is able to lend a hand to the nations that border its territory in the process of establishing a secure environment and cultivating favorable conditions for the growth of economies in the provinces that are engaged. In a practical sense, the BRI may contribute to the improvement of the economic conditions of adjacent countries, which can concurrently diminish terrorist activities and strengthen the security of commerce. Another factor to take into account is the manner in which China cultivates its crops. Throughout history, the rising power has inevitably been involved in a bloody conflict with the established power, such as the United States or the United Kingdom. China seeks to dispel this reputation by rising to power in a manner that is peaceful and does not involve any conflicts. Hence, the BRI is a solution to allay the fears of other nations while also providing them with advantages.

4.2 Theoretical Explanation for China's Motivation

There are a few hypotheses that might be advanced in order to justify China's BRI plan and explain its further intentions. To begin, the structure of Chinese import and export items is analyzed with the use of the theory of intra-industry trade. According to the statistics for the top 8 exporting industries, the Motor Vehicle and Components industry is in fifth position. This industry has an exporting amount of $74 billion and an importing amount of $75 billion, both of which are comparable (Global Edge, 2021). This number implies that the automobile manufacturing business in China is extremely significant and requires a consistent supply; as a result, it must get its supplies from both within and outside of China. In addition, because of globalization and increased specialization, the production of automobiles requires a variety of components that are presently sourced from a large number of nations. Because China is the country in the world that produces the most automobiles, it has a strong incentive to broaden the global market through the Belt and Road Initiative (BRI) in order to both import and export automobiles and their component components.

In addition, the theory of economies of scale can explain why Chinese exporting products have price competitiveness in these years and what kinds of specialization China wants to play in the next new years. This is because economies of scale are based on the idea that larger businesses are more efficient than smaller ones. As was just discussed, economies of scale pertain to situations in which there is a great amount of output. As a result of the employees' rapid improvement along their learning curves and the elements' effective production, the overall cost of each product, on average, is going down. For instance, electrical machinery, which exemplifies to a great extent the comparative advantage of efficient large-scale production, is the category that ranks first among China's exports. But does China wish to continue to specialize in assembling products for sale on the international market in the future? In accordance with the national strategy known as "Made in China 2025," China's goal is to shift the emphasis of its industrial structure from "made in China" to "created in China" and to place more of its attention on the more lucrative aspects of the industrial chain, which are based on front-tier innovations. In this regard, the Belt and Road Initiative (BRI) presents an excellent chance to relocate simple manufacturing to other nations in which the cost of labor is significantly lower.

Several nations, in their efforts to win the worldwide competition, place a strong emphasis on innovation, which they view as the most essential means by which to propel societal development. What does this have to do with the national interest, and why does it matter? This question may be explained using a concept called the technology gap theory. Take for instance the situation presented in Figure 2. The beginning points of three lines of US production, Trade, and British production are different, from T_0, T_1, and T_2, respectively. If the United States was the country that came up with the idea for a new technology and the United Kingdom was the country that accepted it, then the United States would have the competitive advantage of early timing of exporting in the global market, whereas the United Kingdom could only import from the United States until it mastered those particular technical skills and began producing on its own. Because of the disparity in technology, the interval between t_1 and t_3 results in monopoly profits for the country that invents the product. In a similar vein, the year 2019 will see the introduction of 5G technology in China, which was made possible by the "Polar codes" developed by Erdal Arikan, a professor from Turkey. The improvements that are associated with 5G will, without a doubt, provide China with a technical advantage in international trade. As a result, there is a strong impetus to set up a BRI platform in order to take advantage of these benefits.

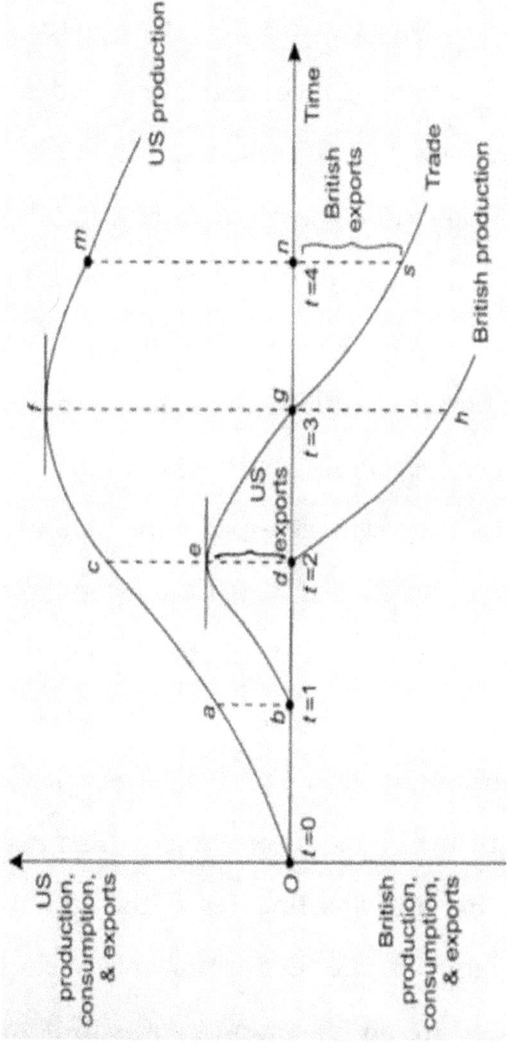

Figure 2: The Model of the Technological Gap.

Every single product goes through the same four stages, which were described in the overview of the theory: the stages of introduction, growth, maturity, and decline. When it is used to international trade, it can be expanded to include five steps in order to describe the many import and export scenarios. As shown in image 3, the rate of growth in exports for nations that are in the stage of invention is rapid during the grow and mature stages, but then it begins to steadily fall until it reaches zero during the decline period. The reduction is explained by some copying of other nations. At the fifth and final stage, the nation that originated the innovation discovers that there are no longer any profits to be made via production. As a result, it decides to begin importing from countries who initially replicated it. In the context of

China, the infrastructure products or services are currently in the stage of 2 and 3 stages; for instance, high railway building; consequently, it is preferable to make as much profit as possible right now before the products step into stage 4 and 5; for example, high railway building. Because of this, China is motivated to submit projects for the Belt and Road Initiative (BRI) in order to further promote its infrastructure - related exports.

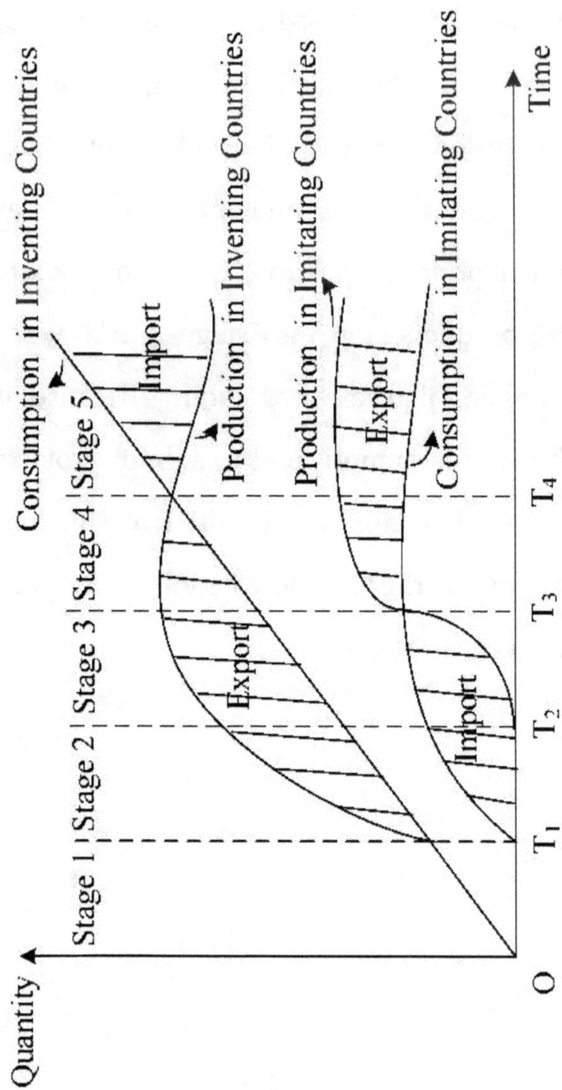

Figure 3: The Model of the Life Cycle Theory.

4.3 The World Context

If we rewind to 2013, the global economy has, for the most part, recovered from the financial crisis that occurred in 2008. Yet, many nations have held the view that globalization should be held responsible for the financial contagion effect, unemployment, immigration, and other factors that culminated in the world financial crisis. When this matter is taken into consideration, trade protectionists all over the world are therefore raised, which results in the trading barrier in the worldwide market being lifted. According to research conducted by the worldwide group Global Trade Alert (GTA) (2019), more than one thousand different protectionist measures have been put into place around the world since 2008. In this scenario, despite the fact that the global economy has begun to recover from the financial crisis of 2008, growth in the world economy remains sluggish, having declined since 2010 and remaining stable at roughly 3% in 2013 (GTA, 2019). At the same time, the conventional model of development, which is based on natural resources and labor costs that are relatively inexpensive, is not appropriate for the current period, which places a greater emphasis on environmental concerns. So, the growth of the globe is in dire need of innovative approaches that are both sustainable and collaborative.

Inequality is another pressing issue that has to be addressed in the context of global development. According to the profile of the globe, certain nations, such as those in

Northern Europe, have already entered the post-modernization stage, whilst other countries are still having trouble getting their modernization and industrialization processes off the ground. As a result of historical circumstances, both Asia and Africa were under the control of western powers for an extended period of time. Due to a lack of competent administration, their economies continued to lag behind or even develop in a retrograde manner even after they achieved their independence. In spite of this, these nations have a significant potential for expansion in terms of their factor endowments; provided, of course, that they improve their industrial and infrastructure bases.

When China is seen in the context of the rest of the globe, it is clear that in 2013, the

United States perceived China as a danger and used economic sanctions to try to curb China's growth and influence. In addition to this, the global market is witnessing a trend of industrial transfer from China to South Asian countries like India and Vietnam as a result of the growing cost of labor. These countries are located in South Asia. China has to take the initiative to seek out possibilities to collaborate with other nations and should do so actively. Nevertheless, According to the BRI materials, the nations of Asia have extremely high transportation costs, which typically account for 30–40% of the total cost of commodities. This share accounts for just 3%-8% of the total expenditures of shipping products throughout European countries, which is a relatively small amount. Based on these findings, it appears that there is an immediate need for improvements to be made to the transportation links that exist between the nations that make up Asia in order for them to be competitive on the global market. As a result, the proposal for the BRI is connected to these different motives.

In a nutshell, this section provides an overview of the background of the BRI in relation to China and the backdrop of the rest of the globe. In light of what has been said thus far, it is not unreasonable to assert that China does, in fact, have a particular demand and the financial capability to initiate BRI. Concurrently, ongoing participation in international trade is essential to the sustained growth of the global economy.

This page intentionally left blank.

5. The Overall Framework of BRI

An "international community with common interests, destiny, and responsibilities" is one of the goals that BRI had for its initiative. It is created with the five objectives of the Belt and Road Initiative (BRI), which are "Political dialogue, Facilities connection, Unimpeded trade, Financial integration, and People-to-people connectivity." The purpose of this design is to accomplish the aim stated above. For connection, numerous modes of transportation need to be constructed and improved, with the goal of achieving the following six transporting targets: integrated information networks in the railway, highway, shipping, aviation, and pipeline systems. To be more exact, the Belt and Road Initiative (BRI) is not a single road but rather an interconnected structure that includes six economic corridors, as depicted in the photos below. Throughout these corridors, as of November 2021, there were over 200 cooperation papers signed between China and other 141 nations and 32 international organizations to collaboratively establish the BRI. Cooperation is taking place in a wide variety of fields in addition to those pertaining to infrastructure. These fields include agriculture, life sciences, information technology, environmental protection, new energy, education, aviation, aerospace, and other related fields.

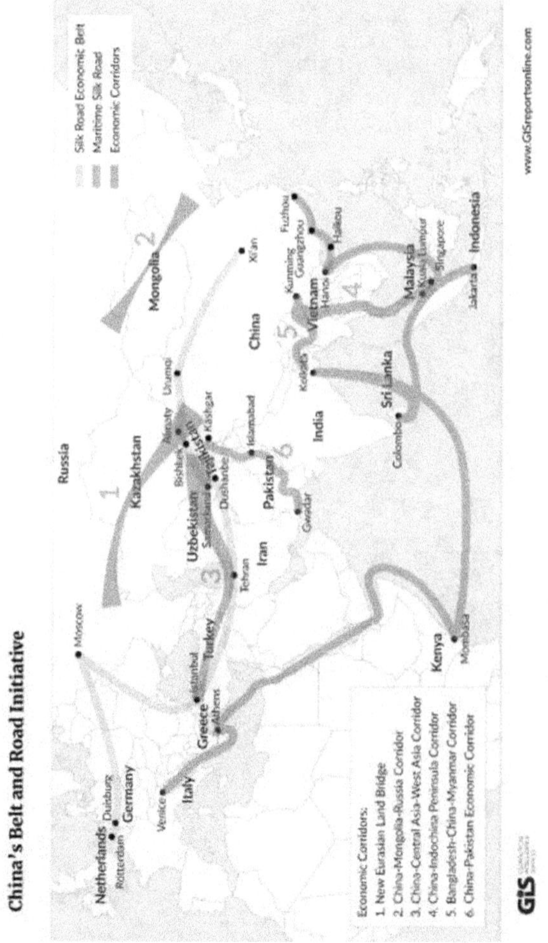

Figure 4: Six Economic Corridors of BRI.
Source: GIS report (2014)

This page intentionally left blank.

6. Review of BRI's Economic Impact

The Belt and Road Initiative (BRI) is a large worldwide endeavor that has gained a lot of interest, as well as critical debates and discussions regarding its potential effects on the economy. In the international community, there are voices that are supportive of this idea, and there are voices that are dubious of this point. On the one hand, the British government has stated that it is interested in increasing the amount of commerce and collaboration that takes place after Brexit, showing its strong support for the BRI initiative (Haenle, 2019). If it is effectively handled and exploited, Russia views the Belt and Road Initiative (BRI) as more of an opportunity than a danger (Haenle, 2019). The European Union communicated to China and the rest of the world in a somewhat ambiguous manner that it wants to be more active and less isolated (Haenle, 2019). Germany has stated that a number of European Union nations want to participate in the BRI as a group (Haenle, 2019). According to Bill Gates, the mentality of being "inward-looking" in the context of economic competitiveness poses a threat to the growth of the world economy (Haenle, 2019). In this regard, he lauded the Belt and Road Initiative (BRI) as a worldwide endeavor that will make many nations more open and engaged.

On the other side, the United States of America is against the Belt and Road Initiative (BRI) and has called for other nations to boycott it because it believes that BRI is a means by which China may expand its geopolitical influence (Curran, 2016). It also pointed out that the Belt and Road Initiative (BRI) has the potential to generate debt entrapment, and that when nations are unable to repay their obligations, they risk losing their autonomy. Certain media outlets in the United States have gone so far as to compare the Belt and Road Initiative (BRI) to a Chinese "Marshall Plan" and have called on the United States government to compete with Beijing by outlining its own infrastructure plan (Curran, 2016). Afghanistan expressed the same concerns on debt, stating that it will not accept any loan under the BRI and will instead accept assistance (Sharma, 2020). Because the Australian government views its bilateral relations with China as being negative, it has decided to cancel two BRI missions (Kuang et al, 2021). In addition, India has been quite critical of the BRI, particularly with regard to the weight of debt and the level of openness. It is so stubborn that it won't even take part in the Second BRI Submit. In addition, India has voiced its displeasure with the China-Pakistan economic corridor concerns the contentious region of "Kashmir" (Hindusstan Times, 2017). Another significant actor, the European Union, continues to present a contradictory stance by stating that it prefers to focus on implementing its own infrastructure plan rather than participating in the Belt and Road Initiative (BRI) because it believes that the BRI would put EU businesses in jeopardy (Haenle, 2019). Because of these worries, the European Union (EU) has just recently revealed its backup plan, which is called the Belt and Road Initiative (BRI) and is an acronym for the phrase "Global Gate." This plan aims to improve the EU's trade and supply chain by investing approximately 300 billion euros in the building of various infrastructure projects (News7H, 2021).

Academic institutions have conducted in-depth research on the BRI's economic impact, which has resulted in the quantifiable impact being based on a variety of economic models. This research was conducted from the viewpoint of the scientific community. For instance, Herrero and Xu (2016) have taken into consideration the three modes of transportation—air, railway, and marine—while applying a gravity model to the setting of international trade. These modes are as follows: air, railway, and maritime. By simulating the connections between these various modes of transportation, they were able to arrive at the conclusion that the BRI would be beneficial for European nations, particularly landlocked ones, under the circumstances of increased global commerce and improved infrastructure (Herrero & Xu, 2016). The team of the World Bank conducted an analysis of the projected infrastructure developments as well as the directions of related gain flows. They discovered that more than fifty percent of the proposed infrastructure projects would result in considerable benefits (Reed & Trubetskoy, 2019). Benefits gained from market access are anticipated to flow into countries with low incomes, whereas benefits generated from projects are anticipated to go into nations with high incomes (Reed & Trubetskoy, 2019). So, various nations will pursue their BRI objectives using a variety of strategies to achieve their goals. Baniya, Rocha, and Ruta (2020) obtained the consistent finding that the BRI will provide good economic consequences to along nations and quantified the increased trade flows, which were found to be as high as 4.1%. They also remark that if trade changes were accompanied by improvements in infrastructure, the measurable impacts would, on average, increase by a factor of three if these two factors were combined. As a result of reading this article, we now understand that advancements in trade policy are just as crucial as those in transportation.

An important piece of study that was carried out by Zhai (2018) makes use of an all-encompassing global computable general equilibrium (CGE) model to predict the BRI's effects on the economy. The author of the study bases his conclusions on the cautious estimates of investing $1.4 trillion into infrastructure between the years 2015 and 2030. The author continued their research and came to the conclusion that the BRI nations as a whole are expected to see yearly profits of $1.5 trillion, which is equivalent to 2.9% of their GDP. The benefits, which are estimated to equal to $1.5 trillion using the price index from 2011, accurately represent the increased production and improved productivity. The author also makes projections on the potential effects of the BRI in the year 2030. The research suggests that by the year 2030, the infrastructure accumulations in all BRI nations and territories, with the exception of China, would have increased by 6-7%. It is anticipated that trade between countries participating in the BRI will expand by 11% as a result of both imports and exports, contributing to an overall increase in global commerce of 5%.

In a summary, the literature indicated that the Belt and Road Initiative (BRI) has a positive impact on the economies of the countries that are connected to it. However, the literature also indicated that the extents of benefits for countries are not even, depending on the amount of economic cooperation that is signed and the amount of financial investments that are injected.

7. Interpretation

To summarize the previous literature assessment, the Belt and Road Initiative (BRI) will undoubtedly have a favorable influence on China's economy as well as the economies of other BRI nations; however, the magnitude of that impact will be determined by a careful weighing of all the relevant factors. The potential and the problems that come with these dynamics go hand in hand. In this section, we will examine the additional factors that BRI has taken into consideration about the economic effect, problems, and future outlooks.

7.1 Other Considerations of BRI Economic Impacts

Although the plan for the BRI has been gradually put into effect in recent era, not all initiatives are open and transparent in the public resources that are available. In addition, there are a great deal of talks that are now taking place. As a result, it is challenging to get an accurate picture of the BRI's scope and investments. Due to the fact that the BRI website is currently undergoing maintenance, there is no information on the beginning or end dates of any of the individual projects. As a consequence of the fact that some BRI projects are not yet operational at the present time, it is hard for ongoing research to provide an accurate evaluation of the level of economic impact that the BRI will have on nations participating in the initiative. All of the current research is carried out based on a variety of hypotheses and conceptual frameworks. These estimates are helpful, but it is not yet known whether or not they are accurate when applied to the real world.

The broad expectation is that the BRI will make cooperative commercial activity more active by increasing the number of possible connection points. The degree of interconnectedness that exists between many nations is unique in its scope. Even if everything goes according to plan with the

Belt and Road Initiative (BRI), many nations will nonetheless experience varying degrees of negative economic effects from the project. To put it another way, nations along the BRI will reap benefits, although in an uneven manner. In Pakistan, for instance, if one were to exclude the cost-cutting and energy-saving effects of infrastructure investment, the country's gross domestic product (GDP) would be increased by 2.7%. In spite of this, Turkey's percentage comes in at 0.7% (Zhai, 2018).

It should come as no surprise that infrastructure bonds may significantly cut transaction costs. Yet, there are many building pieces in the relationship between the improvement of infrastructure and the lowering of costs. For instance, the speed of customs checks and support for trading policies are two of these building blocks. In a same vein, the usage of related technologies and the introduction of new sources of energy are required in order to achieve sustainable levels of energy consumption along the BRI nations. Consequently, the BRI is not only an enhancement to the infrastructure; rather, it is a holistic network that necessitates the deliberate reconciliation of politics, culture, society, business, and any and all other associated areas.

7.2 Challenges

Because of the diversity of the countries involved, international collaboration has always been fraught with difficulties. This has been the case for several decades. The BRI is not, of course, an exception to this rule. The fundamental reason why the Belt and Road Initiative (BRI) confronts a huge number of obstacles is that the nations that make up the route have major differences. For instance, because the bulk of the countries that the BRI passes through are still in the process of economic development, and because many of those nations lack dependable institutions and a secure environment. Because there have been more or less political tremors and upheavals, the political dangers are rather significant. Also, it is anticipated that the BRI framework would handle a number of global challenges, such as those pertaining to environmental preservation and climate change, for example. In addition to problems that are particular to individual nations, the Belt and Road Initiative (BRI) needs additional improvements in terms of its transparency and its capacity to remain sustainable.

BRI is now confronted with two main difficulties that it has identified and is working to overcome. To begin, the topic that has received the greatest criticism from the international community is connected with the debt trap, owing to the fact that investments made through BRI are not completely free of risk, but do incur the financial costs of interests. Because a significant number of BRI nations have investment rates that are far lower than what is considered to be fair, the OECD analysis concludes that the Belt and Road Initiative (BRI) poses a high level of economic risk. The baseline for investments that are advised is a BBB- rating, and credit rates are often adjusted to reflect an individual nation's capacity to repay its debts. According to the data that follows, just 17 of the nations that are a part of the BRI have achieved a credit rating of BBB- or above, 29 economies have a rating that is worse than BBB-, and 14 countries do not have any credit ratings at all. As a result, there is a significant possibility that the debt owing to the BRI financial foundation by the nations who participated in the BRI would not be reimbursed. This is a pressing issue that has to be addressed by the Belt and Road Initiative (BRI), perhaps through a variety of financial instruments, in order to boost the credibility and confidence of BRI projects.

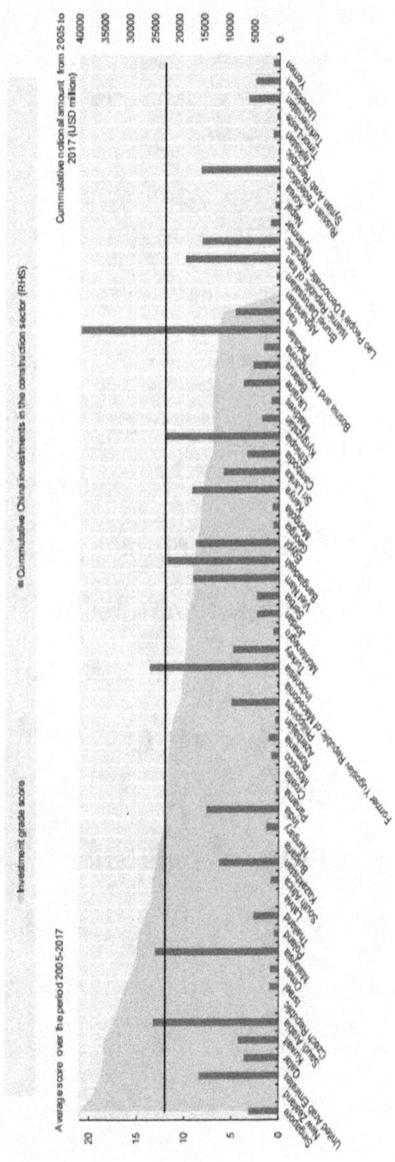

Figure 5: Credit Rate of BRI Countries throughout 2005-2017.

Note: Normally, AAA and Aaa are given a score of 21; AA+ and Aa1 are given a score of 20; Investment grade ends at BBB-/Baa3 at a score of 12. down to 1 for D and C at the junk end.

Second, as the ongoing COVID-19 pandemic continues to worsen, the economic issues that were caused by the "stagflation" that followed the financial crisis of 1970 are expected to reappear. When economic expansion is sluggish, unemployment rates are high, and prices continue to rise all at the same time, this is referred to as a perfect storm (Bruno & Sachs, 2013). Why is it likely that the epidemic will cause stagflation? There are two primary explanations for this. As a consequence of the epidemic, there is now insufficient supply of both products and services, as well as labor. At the same time, ineffective fiscal and monetary policies have led to a surplus of money that is in excess of what is required for the economy. Under this scenario, worldwide trade, including the BRI project, would be negatively impacted by sluggish customs clearance processes, restricted trading flows, and a disorganized global supply chain.

7.3 Outlook

On the basis of what has been discussed thus far, it is not difficult for us to envision what the BRI should be adamant about and what its goals for the future would be. In the first place, in order for the Belt and Road Initiative (BRI) to accomplish its goals, it is required to adhere steadfastly to its guiding principles, which are "Open, Intelligence, Innovation, Health, Green,

Prosperity and Peace." By participation in a variety of conferences, countries should work to improve their mutual knowledge of one another. In addition, in order to win the trust of countries, the Belt and Road Initiative (BRI) needs to be compatible with the national strategies of a variety of countries. This will allow them to search for areas of common interest, such as the EU-Eurasian plan, Mongolia's "Prairie Road," Turkey-Middle Corridor, Russia-Eurasian Economic Union (EEU), etc. In terms of developments in the future, there is a tendency for BRI to concentrate on the aspects that solve the concerns that are shared by all parties. To be more particular, the prospective areas for greater collaboration include air, education, green, technology, smart, and digital BRI.

Turkey, which has been a significant nation from ancient to current times, possesses a great deal of competitive edge in the international market. As a result, it is essential to bring up the prospective partnerships that might be formed between China and Turkey within the BRI framework. According to Kocakolu et al (2020)'s research, Turkey possesses exceptional geographical advantages that allow it to reach the markets of Europe, the Middle East, and North Africa. When compared to China's labor cost, Turkey's labor cost is considerably cheaper. In addition, in order to entice foreign direct investment, Turkey has implemented a system of tax reductions and exemptions for corporations as part of its incentive program. Because of its domestic circumstances, Turkey enjoys significant advantages in the industries of textile production, manufacturing, and the production of agricultural goods (Oz, 2002). The potential for collaboration between Turkey and China is greatly expanded as a result of these advantages.

More importantly, Turkey only recently developed the "industry 4.0 plan," which shares the same goal as China's "Made in China 2025" strategy in terms of the enhancement of the Information and Communication Technologies (ICT) business (Erboz, 2020). So, there is a significant opportunity for Turkey and China to collaborate closely in this field, despite the fact that a portion of this opportunity has already been achieved in practice. For instance, over one hundred Chinese businesses have established themselves in Turkey. These businesses range from those in the financial sector like Bank of China to those in the research and development sector like Huawei and Turkcell. As a result of this pattern, increased collaboration is forecasted to take place in the years to come.

This page intentionally left blank.

8. Conclusion

It should not come as a surprise that China first proposed the BRI in 2013. This global initiative, which draws its inspiration from the historic trade routes known as silk roads, has as its primary goal the improvement of communication between various nations. When seen through the prism of China's national interest, we discover that the country possesses a unique history as well as unique motives to push for the BRI in the global environment of 2013. In order to understand the fundamental causes for BRI, many explanations, such as "overlapped demand," "technology gap," and "product life cycle," are brought into play. After looking over the relevant research, we came to the conclusion that if the BRI is effectively put into action, it will have a significant, if uneven, influence on the economies of the many nations involved. In general, it will make it easier for producing components to move from one country to another, maximizing the allocation of resources throughout the world, and eventually fostering equality and common wealth on a global scale. On the other hand, obstacles are invariably there whenever opportunity exist. The BRI nations still need to face the primary issues, which include the mistrust of the international community, a potential debt crisis, and stagflation brought on by COVID-19. These problems may be solved by collaboration and reconciliation.

Appendix: Take-away of BRI Evolution

This part is taken from the presentation made by Yunxin Chang at the Istanbul Commerce University seminar. The seminar was chaired by Prof. Dr. Üyesi Cihat Köksal.

Yunxin Chang showed the evolution and development process of BRI through slides, and answered questions raised by scholars from Iran, Germany, Uganda, etc.

What are the BRI's vision, objective and framework?

Evolution of BRI

BRI Vision: To establish an "international community with shared interests, destiny, and responsibility"

BELT and ROAD
一带一路

5 Objectives:
Political Dialogue, Facilities Connectivity, Unimpeded Trade, Financial Integration, People-to-people connectivity

6 Means of Transportations:
Railway, Highway, Shipping, Aviation,Pipeline and Space integrated information network.

6 economic corridors:
(1)New Eurasian Land Bridge; (2) the China-Mongolia-Russia Economic Corridor;(3) the China–Central Asia–West Asia Economic Corridor; (4) the China–Indochina Peninsula Economic Corridor; (5) theBangladesh-China-India-Myanmar Economic Corridor; (6) the China-Pakistan Economic Corridor.

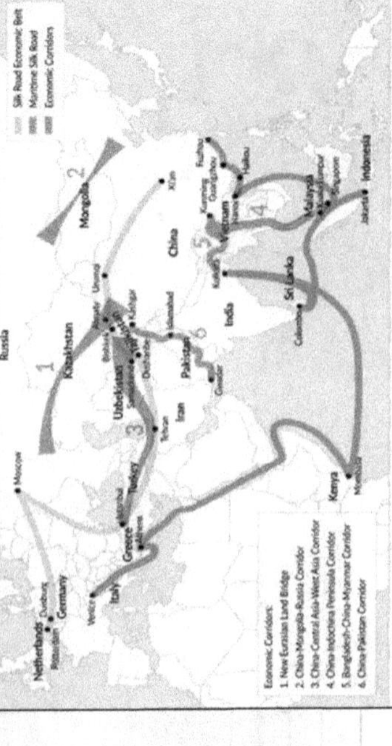

Figure A1.

Evolution of BRI
Who is funding BRI?
In 2014, the establishment of the **BRICS Bank for Reconstruction and Development** was announced, and a reserve fund of **100 billion US dollars** was established. Included countries are Brazil, Russia, India, China, South Africa.
On 8 Nov., 2014, Xi Jinping announced that China will invest **40 billion** U.S. dollars to establish the **Silk Road Fund**, which will provide infrastructure, resource development, industrial cooperation and financial services for countries along the BRI. In 2017, Xi Jinping announced **another 100 billion** yuan increase in the fund.
On 25 Dec.2015, the **Asian Infrastructure Investment Bank(AIIB)**, led by China and jointly prepared by 57 countries including United Kingdom, France, Italy, Germany and other countries covering five continents, was formally established. This is the first multilateral financial institution initiated by China in the world. It has headquater in Beijing and legal cpital of **100 billion US dollars**.
New Development Bank
丝路基金
Silk Road Fund
AIIB
ASIAN INFRASTRUCTURE
INVESTMENT BANK

Figure A2.

How BRI enrich and envolve itself?

Evolution of BRI

Air BRI

- In 2017, the leaders of China and Luxembourg has agree to have a direct flight connecting them, which is "Zhengzhou-Luxembourg" flight line.
- It is now under building and be will put into operation in 2025.
- More cooperations in the flight areas will be reached.

Education BRI

- In 2016, China has issued the action plan "Promoting the Joint Construction of BRI Education Action".
- Provides 10,000 government scholarships to BRI countries each year to improve mutual understanding.

Green BRI

- Establishing green BRI and stop investing any oversea polluted projects in 2017.
- Example: Morago Hakanda Irrigation Project in Sri Lanka, providing not only irrigation but clean drinking water
- "China's 2030 Agenda of Sustainable Development"
- Energy-saving, low-carbon and renewable projects along BRI.

Figure A3.

How BRI enrich and envolve itself?

Evolution of BRI

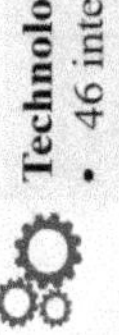

Technological BRI

- 46 intergovernmental science and technology cooperation agreements with BRI countries
- Covere agriculture, life sciences, IT, environmental protection, new energy, aerospace etc.
- Establish scientific and technological platforms such as joint laboratories, international technology transfer centers, and science and technology parks.

Smart BRI

- In 2005, BRI International Think Tank Cooperation Committee was established. This pools knowledges into the development of BRI.
- 15 countries' think tank has joined.

Digital BRI

- "China wants to intensify co-operation in frontier areas such as digital economy, artificial intelligence, nanotechnology and quantum computing, and advance the development of big data, cloud computing and smart cities so as to turn them into a digital silk road of the 21st century." (Xi, J., 2017a)
- In 2015, China has reached cooperation with London International Mobile Company, which provides global communications and positioning services by 12 satellites covering the world, to ensure instant communication in remote areas along BRI countries.

Figure A4.

Evolution of BRI
Example cases of BRI
1. China Railway Express(CRE)
An important and innevitable component of BRI, creating logistics channel between China and Europe countries, Milan, Moscow, Minsk, Hamburg, etc.
Develop rapidly since the first train in 2011, from 17 trains per year in 2011 to 6363 in 2018 (Zhao, Cheng, Li and Hu, 2019)
One of the CRE train uses Istanbul's subsea Marmaray railway tunnel to cross into Europe

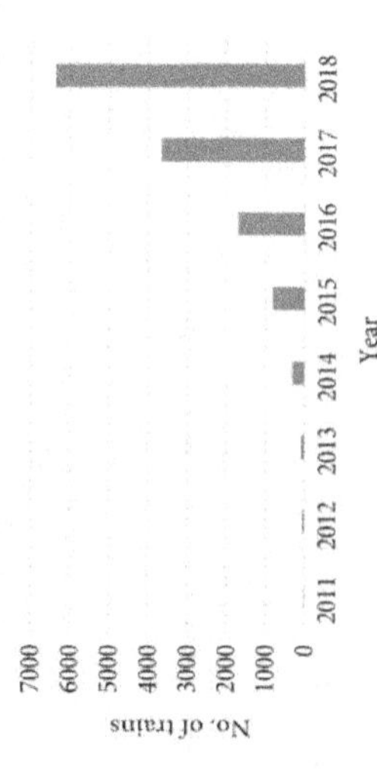
No. of trains
7000
6000
5000
4000
3000
2000
1000
0
2011
2012
2013
2014
2015
2016
2017
2018
Year

2. Ankara-Istanbul Highspeed Railway in Turkey
The high railway train between Akara and Istanbul is joint built by China and other two Turkish companies. China has provided partly financial support. The speed of the train can reach up to 250km/h. The transporting time is largely reduced from almost 6 hours to 3 hours.

Figure A5.

Example cases of BRI

3. Pakistan QA photovoltaic power

- Lead by China company ZTE Energy and jointly build with local companies
- Helps to utilize solar energy
- Now partly used and partly under construction
- After the completion, become the world's largest single photovoltaic power generation project.

Evolution of BRI

4. The Port of Piraeus in Greek

- Become the biggest port for Greek and fourth biggest prot in Europe.
- Includes trading and transportation hub
- Be useful for prosperity of Greek and trade between China and Europe, good in both way. (Greek Prime Minister George Papandreou, 2021)

Figure A6.

Evolution of BRI

As of November 2021, China has signed more than 200 cooperation documents for jointly building the BRI with **141 countries** and **32 international organizations**. The following table is the initial joint countries in 2015.

	Economy	Economic Corridor		Economy	Economic Corridor
1	People's Republic of China	-	37	Singapore	China-Indochina Peninsula
2	Bangladesh	Bangladesh-China-India-Myanmar	38	Thailand	China-Indochina Peninsula
3	Bhutan	Bangladesh-China-India-Myanmar	39	Timor-Leste	China-Indochina Peninsula
4	India	Bangladesh-China-India-Myanmar	40	Viet Nam	China-Indochina Peninsula
5	Myanmar	Bangladesh-China-India-Myanmar	41	Belarus	China-Mongolia-Russian Federation
6	Nepal	Bangladesh-China-India-Myanmar	42	Estonia	China-Mongolia-Russian Federation
7	Sri Lanka	Bangladesh-China-India-Myanmar	43	Latvia	China-Mongolia-Russian Federation
8	Albania	China-Central West Asia	44	Lithuania	China-Mongolia-Russian Federation
9	Armenia	China-Central West Asia	45	Mongolia	China-Mongolia-Russian Federation
10	Azerbaijan	China-Central West Asia	46	Russian Federation	China-Mongolia-Russian Federation
11	Bosnia and Herzegovina	China-Central West Asia	47	Afghanistan	China-Pakistan
12	Bulgaria	China-Central West Asia	48	Pakistan	China-Pakistan
13	Croatia	China-Central West Asia	49	Bahrain	China-Pakistan
14	Georgia	China-Central West Asia	50	Kuwait	China-Pakistan
15	Islamic Republic of Iran	China-Central West Asia	51	Oman	China-Pakistan
16	Iraq	China-Central West Asia	52	Qatar	China-Pakistan
17	Israel	China-Central West Asia	53	Saudi Arabia	China-Pakistan
18	Jordan	China-Central West Asia	54	United Arab Emirates	China-Pakistan
19	Kyrgyzstan	China-Central West Asia	55	Yemen	China-Pakistan
20	Lebanon	China-Central West Asia	56	Czech Republic	New Eurasian Land Bridge
21	Former Yugoslav Republic of Macedonia	China-Central West Asia	57	Hungary	New Eurasian Land Bridge
22	Republic of Moldova	China-Central West Asia	58	Slovak Republic	New Eurasian Land Bridge
23	Montenegro	China-Central West Asia	59	Slovenia	New Eurasian Land Bridge
24	Palestinian Authority or West Bank and Gaza Strip	China-Central West Asia	60	Poland	New Eurasian Land Bridge
25	Romania	China-Central West Asia	61	Kazakhstan	New Eurasian Land Bridge
26	Serbia	China-Central West Asia	62	Ukraine	New Eurasian Land Bridge
27	Syrian Arab Republic	China-Central West Asia	63	Egypt	21st-C Maritime Silk Road
28	Tajikistan	China-Central West Asia	64	Ethiopia	21st-C Maritime Silk Road
29	Turkey	China-Central West Asia	65	Indonesia	21st-C Maritime Silk Road
30	Turkmenistan	China-Central West Asia	66	Kenya	21st-C Maritime Silk Road
31	Uzbekistan	China-Central West Asia	67	Maldives	21st-C Maritime Silk Road
32	Brunei Darussalam	China-Indochina Peninsula	68	Morocco	21st-C Maritime Silk Road
33	Cambodia	China-Indochina Peninsula	69	New Zealand	21st-C Maritime Silk Road
34	Lao People's Democratic Republic	China-Indochina Peninsula	70	Panama	21st-C Maritime Silk Road
35	Malaysia	China-Indochina Peninsula	71	Korea	21st-C Maritime Silk Road
36	Philippines	China-Indochina Peninsula	72	South Africa	21st-C Maritime Silk Road

Theory of Overlapping Demands

- Most BRI countries are developing countries that share the silimar economic conditions.
- The demanding will be overlapped.
- This theory explains fundamental reason why BRI includes so many developing countries and why trading among them is a possible.

Source: OECD Business and Finance outlook, 2018

Figure A7.

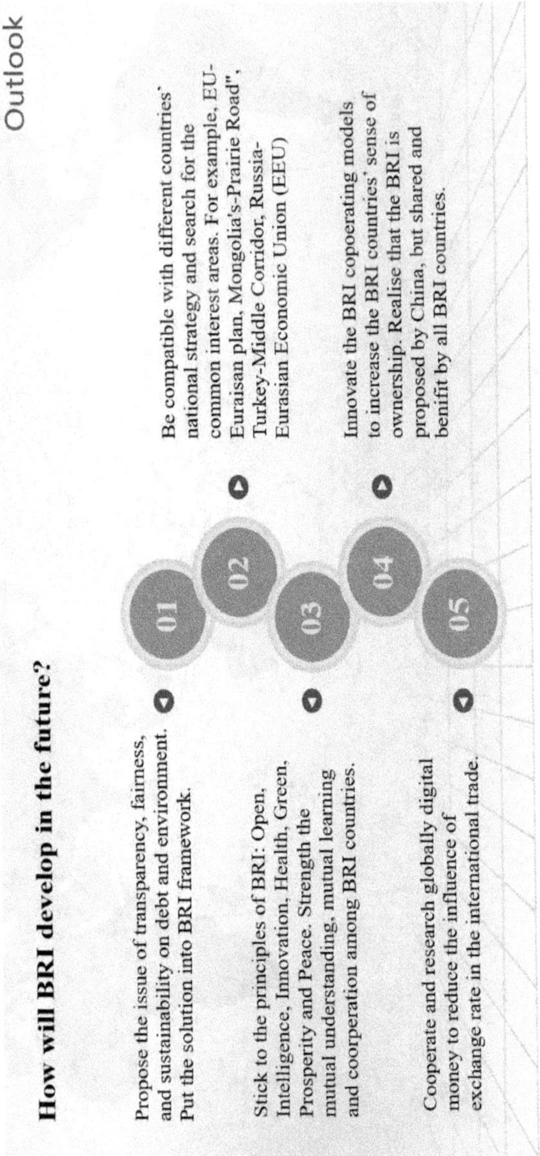

Outlook

How will BRI develop in the future?

01

Propose the issue of transparency, fairness, and sustainability on debt and environment. Put the solution into BRI framework.

02

Be compatible with different countries' national strategy and search for the common interest areas. For example, EU-Euraisan plan, Mongolia's-Prairie Road", Turkey-Middle Corridor, Russia-Eurasian Economic Union (EEU)

03

Stick to the principles of BRI: Open, Intelligence, Innovation, Health, Green, Prosperity and Peace. Strength the mutual understanding, mutual learning and coorperation among BRI countries.

04

Innovate the BRI copoerating models to increase the BRI countries' sense of ownership. Realise that the BRI is proposed by China, but shared and benifit by all BRI countries.

05

Cooperate and research globally digital money to reduce the influence of exchange rate in the international trade.

Figure A8.

Reference

Bao, X. (2013). Exploring a road to ecological transformation of industrial parks. *China Economic Daily*. Retrieved from http://www.bda.gov.cn/cms/mtjj/80668.htm

Baniya, S., Rocha, N., & Ruta, M. (2020). Trade effects of the New Silk Road: A gravity analysis. *Journal of Development Economics*, 146, 102467.

Bruno, M., & Sachs, J. D. (2013). *Economics of worldwide stagflation*. Harvard University Press.

Chin, T. (2013). The invention of the Sil

k Road, 1877. *Critical Inquiry*, 40(1), 194-219.

Curran. E. (2016). China's Marshall plan. *Bloomberg*. Retrieved from https://www.bloomberg.com/news/articles/2016-08-07/china-s-marshall-plan

Dong. X, R, (2019). Naming of the Silk Road. In *Routledge Handbook of the Belt and Road* (pp. 53-56). Routledge.

Erboz, E. (2020). A Qualitative Study on Industry 4.0 Competitiveness in Turkey Using Porter Diamond Model. *Journal of Industrial Engineering and Manageme nt*, 13(2), 266-282

Guan, K. C. (2016). The maritime silk ro ad: history of an idea. *NSC Working Pa per.* 23, 1-20.

Guo, X, G. (2014). The background and significance of the “One Belt One Road” initiative. Retrieved from https://www.ci is.org.cn/ydylyjzx/zfsj/202009/t20200923_7 496.html

Global Trade Alert (GTA). (2019). Anti-gl obalisation and its effect on supply chai ns. Retrieved from https://www.incegd.com/en/news-insights/commodities-trade-anti-globalisation-and-its-effect-supply-chains

Global Edge. Database. (2021). China export and import data by industries. Retrieved from https://globaledge.msu.edu/countries/china/tradestats

Heston. A, Sicular. T, Brandt. L, Rawski, G. Thomas. (2008). *China's great economic transformation.* Cambridge University Press. pp. 27 - 67. https://doi.org/10.1017/CBO9780511754234.003

Haenle. P, Ternin. D. Gabuev A. Baruah, M.D., Feng, Y, Ma, B. (2019, Apr. 25). How are various countries responding to China's Belt and Road Initiative? Retrieved from https://carnegieendowment.org/2019/04/25/how-are-various-countries-responding-to-china-s-belt-and-road-initiative-pub-79002

Hindusstan Times. (2017, May, 25). CPEC route through Kashmir could create tension with India: UN report. Retrieved from https://www.hindustantimes.com/world-news/cpec-route-through-kashmir-could

-create-tension-with-india-un-report/story-05fDgjtdFmATT6K13ZJffN.html

Herrero, A. G., & Xu, J. (2016). China's belt and road initiative: Can Europe expect trade gains? *Bruegel working paper series.* Issue 5.

Juping, Y. (2009). Alexander the great and the emergence of the silk road. *The Silk Road,* 6(2), 15-22.

Kuang, W., Fang, J., Jose, H. (2021, Apr. 22). Australia's move to scrap Victoria-China Belt and Road agreement goes viral on Weibo. https://www.abc.net.au/news/2021-04-22/australia-china-belt-road-initiative-cancellation-viral-weibo/100086594

Koçakoğlu, M. A., Sevinç, M. R., & Cançelik, M. (2020). China's capital export within the through of Belt And Road Initiative: A model application for Turkey. *Research Gate.* Retrieved from https://www.researchgate.net/publication/340815628

Linder, S. B. (1961). An essay on trade and transformation (pp. 82-109). Stockholm: Almqvist & Wiksell.

News7H. (2021. Nov. 29). EU plans to sp end 300 billion euros on global infrastru cture to compete with China. Retrieved from https://news7h.com/eu-plans-to-spe nd-300-billion-euros-on-global-infrastruct ure-to-compete-with-china/

OECD (2018). The Belt and Road Initiati ve in the global trade, investment and fi nance landscape", in *OECD Business and Finance Outlook 2018*, OECD Publishing, Paris, https://doi.org/10.1787/bus_fin_out -2018-6-en.

Öz, Ö. (2002). Assessing Porter's framew ork for national advantage: the case of T urkey. *Journal of Business Research, 55* (6), 509-515.

Palmerston, L. (1848). Treaty of Andrian ople. *Speech to the House of.*

Posner, M.V. (1961). International Trade and Technical Change. *Oxford Economic Papers.* 3, 323-341.

Polo, M. (1986). *The Book of Marco Pol o.* AMS Press.

Ricardo, D. (1891). *Principles of political*

economy and taxation. G. Bell and sons.

Robinson, J. (1969). *The economics of i mperfect competition.* Springer.

Rawski, T. G. (1995). Implications of Chi na'Reform Experience. *The China Quarte rly,* 144, 1150-1173.

Reed, T., & Trubetskoy, A. (2019). Assess ing the value of market access from belt and road projects. *World Bank Policy R esearch Working Paper,* 8815

Smith, A. (1937). *The wealth of nations* [1776], 11937

Scott, M. F. G. (1975). Intra-industry tra de: the theory and measurement of inte rnational trade in differentiated products. 646-648

Stigler, G. J. (1958). The economies of sc ale. *The Journal of Law and Economics,* 1, 54-71

Sharma, P. (2020, Jan, 5). Afghanistan a nd Myanmar drown in China's loans; Af ghanistan rejects loan. Retrieved from ht tps://www.wionews.com/afghanistan/afgha

nistan-and-myanmar-drown-in-chinas-loans-afghanistan-rejects-loan-306145

Vernon, R. (1992). International investment and international trade in the product cycle. In *International economic policies and their theoretical foundations* (pp. 415-435). Academic Press.

World Bank. (2014, Dec, 19). China's High-Speed Rail: the Rapid Growth of a New Travel Option. Retrieved from https://www.worldbank.org/en/news/press-release/2014/12/19/china-high-speed-rail-the-rapid-growth-of-a-new-travel-option

Zhai, F. (2018). China's belt and road initiative: A preliminary quantitative assessment. *Journal of Asian Economics*, 55, 84-92.

Open Democracy
& Stettbach Press

www.ingramcontent.com/pod-product-compliance
Lightning Source LLC
LaVergne TN
LVHW010111170826
845678LV00012B/2347